A Widow's Handbook

Help for navigating the widowhood maze

WENDY CHRISTOPHER

To my extraordinary family, wonderful supportive friends,
but most of all to John who loved me "forever and a day"

A Widow's Handbook

Help for navigating the widowhood maze

print ISBN: 979-8-35093-507-3

ebook ISBN: 979-8-35093-508-0

CONTENTS

PREFACE

It seems as though I have many friends who have lost their husbands in the past few months. Some had been ill and some took the same route my husband did…had a heart attack and died on the spot. Either way, the loss is devastating and the widow is left drifting. I was at a funeral home uttering those words we've all said a million times, "I'm so sorry for your loss" when it dawned on me to add, "it's a shame there isn't a handbook for widows." Now, I was raised to correct a problem if you saw it. You know, if there's a piece of paper on the ground, pick it up, if you see someone who looks lost ask if they need directions; someone is short a dollar at the cash register…give it to them. You get the point. So, here I am writing a handbook for widows.

On September 29, 1971 I met this guy named John. A mutual friend of ours had tried to get us together for a year. This friend was a terrible salesman! He kept telling John that he had just the girl for him. "She's this tall" (imagine him holding out his hand about 4 feet off the ground) "has red hair" (John really disliked red hair!) "And she's crazy!" Wow! If that didn't make John want to meet me, I don't know what would! Roy also kept telling me that he had the perfect guy for me. He was this tall (you guessed it, 4 feet), and bald. Yup, the man of my dreams, a bald midget! No offence to little people every- where, I know it was shallow, but I always dreamed of a guy who was movie star handsome, with full head of dark wavy hair and who towered over me. He would be the guy riding the white horse and saving the princess in every storybook. This dream was over 50 years ago, so I'm not sure if he was wearing a cape and had super powers or not, but he definitely wasn't 5' 7" and bald! On September 29, 1971 Roy finally got us together by inviting me to a concert that the Kiwanis club John and Roy were both in, was sponsoring. John and I looked at each other and fell in love! Really, just like in the movies! Three months later we were engaged and on April 29, 1972, we were married. For those of you who are slightly math challenged, that's exactly seven months after we met. Then, just before our twenty sixth anniversary, on March 21, 1998, John had a heart attack and dropped dead in our driveway. Our two oldest sons were in college, our youngest son living at home, but finding himself, and our daughter was eight days away from turning thirteen.

Not everyone's love story had a happy ending that read, "and they lived happily ever after". Some people reading this book had a marriage that could have been anything from less than ideal to downright awful. If your marriage fell into that group, that's okay, acknowledge it. Just because someone dies, he doesn't automatically become a saint. Let's be honest, some people are just plain terrible people. If you were married to someone like that don't feel guilty for saying so. And certainly, don't think that he was terrible because of something you did or didn't do, that was inside him when you got married and he brought it out, you didn't.

To say that day and all the days, months and years that have followed John's death have been filled with learning experiences, would be an understatement. What you are going to read is a compilation of my own great choices, bad ideas, and things I've heard from or witnessed other widows doing or saying.

Keep in mind when you are reading this that everyone is different and there is no right or wrong, but I can tell you, that you would be surprised that under the surface there are a lot more similarities than differences in the things that happen to each of us and how we react and could react, to those things.

IN THE BEGINNING

When you were first married or became partners, you probably were as much or more in lust than in love, and over time that lust cooled and became more like an old pair of sweat pants, comfortable and reliable; something you couldn't dream of parting with. It was something you could count on to always be there and be the same. While you were married you experienced many, many, things together. Possibly children, trips, financial highs and lows. You probably bought things together, maybe a house, furniture, a car, tchotchkes, a special book, this list could on forever, and I'm sure you could add a hundred items to it without even thinking, but my point is that every one of those things will remind you of him. Each of those items will time warp you back to a memory. Some of those memories will be good and others, maybe not. Accept that the good memories will often bring tears and heartache with them, at least in the beginning. Use the ones that reignite bad memories to help counter your grief. If something brings up a bad or unpleasant memory, get rid of it! Keeping it is like picking at your cuticle, the pain never has a chance to stop. There is no point in torturing yourself.

I DON'T FEEL LIKE
DOING ANYTHING

If someone asks you to go somewhere or do something, GO! DO!

There is more than one reason for this. Right now, you may feel like lying in bed hiding under the covers, but as much as you don't want to hear this, he's gone, but you are not. You still have a life to live, and I promise that if you accept those invitations, eventually, (and I'm not saying tomorrow or the next day), it will feel more like living.

Think of a time when you hurt yourself, maybe an arm or leg, and you favored that part of your body. When you eventually discovered that you really needed both arms to get dressed or both legs to get to the store, you worked that muscle, and it hurt! But, little by little, it stopped hurting, and eventually that severe pain was relegated to memory status. That's what going and doing will do for that severe pain of loss you're feeling right now.

I remember a few weeks after John died, something funny happened. I'm talking about a Carol Burnett skit funny, and I started to laugh. My first feeling was guilt. Why was I laughing? How could I dare to laugh when John was dead and I missed him so much? But then somewhere back in that pea size part of my brain labeled either "Common Sense" or "Self-Centeredness" I realized that it felt good to really (verses polite) laugh and that my body felt good when I laughed. For that one frozen moment, my body stopped hurting. I hadn't even realized how much it was hurting until it stopped and then started up again. But after many more laugh moments the hurt started being moved more to the back and the lightness of life moved forward.

In a way I was fortunate that I had to work, because it forced me to get out. John and I had been living paycheck to paycheck for a very long time. There wasn't any massive insurance policy, in fact there wasn't any insurance policy to carry me along. There wasn't anyone to blame or sue for a huge settlement. Making the mortgage payment, feeding and clothing the children and putting gas in the car wouldn't happen unless I did it. My mother-in-law paid for the funeral (thank you mom), my neighbors collected money for me and my priest handed me a check for $1000. All this was very humbling, as tight as things had been we had always taken care of ourselves, and now I was sending thank you's to friends and neighbors for realizing I was in trouble and I needed help supporting my family. So, the week after burying my beloved husband, I went back to work. I have to be honest; I had a crappy attitude and was actually called into the boss's office and asked if maybe I came back a little too soon. All I could say was that I had to. I had to explain to them that under the company policy I had three days bereavement and then I was on my own; and that was a luxury I literally couldn't afford as much as I would have liked it. As bad as it was going back to work, it was good because it added that layer of normalcy to my life. I know that without going back to the job, I would have been focused on myself and how much I hurt, instead of my children and how much they were also hurting. That job made me get up and get dressed every day. It forced me to talk to people and worry about what I was going to make for dinner, whether I wanted to eat or not. After that conversation with my boss, I also knew that it was giving me an outlet for the anger I was experiencing about how unfair John's death was, even if it wasn't the best outlet.

In the meantime, because friends and family saw me standing upright and getting dressed every day, they invited me to go and do things, and they came to visit. Not every visit is welcome or wanted, and saying that is okay, although you may want to be a little nicer than I was that first Easter.

My mother and brother decided that since John had only been gone a few weeks that we, my children and I, should have company for Easter. Normally this was a happy event. Let's be honest, wherever there is chocolate, there's usually happiness, and in our house, Easter was an all-chocolate day. I'd have baskets brimming with everyone's favorite treat and of course a chocolate dessert. We could be on a sugar high for days! Anyway, Mother and Brian told me that they were coming for Easter, and Brian would be bringing his wife and daughter. What would I like them to bring? Nothing. Don't come and don't bring anything. They responded by asking what time we would be eating. What part of I didn't want them to come didn't they understand? How dense are these people? Well, not getting the hint they showed up for dinner with dishes and more candy. As we sat around the table giving praise for all we had and were about to eat, I contained myself. But, as the conversation swirled around me, I grew more and more enraged and my children grew more and more quiet. I don't know if they were reading my mood, or if they were feeling the same as I was, but finally I'd had enough. I lost it! As I was leaving the table in tears, I told them how much I didn't want them there in no uncertain terms. Fortunately, they are my family and were very forgiving and supportive of what I wanted and didn't want, in the future. There are going to be times you are going to lose it. Hopefully it will be in private. Whether public or private, when you do, forgive yourself. You are the one with the open wound like a gash. The only way that wound will heal is by being out with people. You will still miss your partner, but the pain will ease faster and better with others around you.

WHAT HAPPENED TO MY FRIENDS?

One thing that was pointed out to me recently is that a widow's social circle changes dramatically when your title changes from "wife" to "widow". You will find that since you're not part of a couple any longer, you tend to be excluded from couple's events. The gal I was talking to and I discussed this at length and weren't able to decide if you are excluded because other women, no matter how close you have been to them in the past, don't want you around their husbands or if they are truly thinking of your feelings and don't want to add to your misery by seeing other people paired off. I think it's probably a little of each, but whatever the cause, you aren't there with your friends. And at the times you are included, you suddenly know exactly what a fifth wheel is. Neither being included, nor being excluded feels good. Other widows may ask you to join them going to dinner or maybe the movies, but even this will feel strange, particularly if they aren't people you would have done these things with in the past.

John and I were friends with a couple for many years. Our families often got together for pot-luck dinners; we spent Easters together and volunteered at the same projects. We were one of the first to be told that their daughter was expecting and later that Ibby had a malignant, non-operable, tumor in his brain. It was a long few years from when he was diagnosed to when he passed. John and I were close enough to them that we were actually with him when he died. After his death, Marilyn, his widow, pulled away from us. For a long time, I thought I had done something to offend her, but in writing this book, I realize that it hurt her too much to be near us. We brought back too many memories and were left in a past that she didn't want to have dredged up. I like to think that I didn't do that to others, but, if I did, I know now that it is a natural occurrence.

YOU CAN COMBAT SAD

It's OK to be sad. Understand that a memory, a particular smell, some silly thing that someone says or does, some item or an incident will make you sad and maybe even cry. That's alright, and people do understand. You will have a few who don't and who will tell you to try to just move on, but you need to understand that there isn't a way to just move on and also grieve the way you need to. That being said, if it were the other way around and you were the one who died, how would you want your spouse or partner to handle it? Would you want them to make it their life's work to be sad and unhappy? Would you want them to go looking for things that they know would make them sad? My guess is, no, you wouldn't. You would want them to do things that make them smile and feel if not happy, at least not sad.

After John died, I realized pretty quickly, that this was going to happen. I did make a conscious effort to not put myself in a position that could trigger those memories and the melancholy that came on then. Fortunately, as I've said before, I wasn't in a position to withdraw from life, but you can continue and appear fairly normal. You will find that there are big triggers, and little ones. The little ones are the worse, and really blindside you, but the big ones you can avoid. For example, there was a show, The Muppets, that our whole family watched every week. For me, that show was a big trigger. The first time it came on, I left the room to go do the dinner dishes or fold laundry. These were normal tasks and I don't think the kids noticed or realized how much just hearing the opening music upset me. I could never watch that show again after John died. Another time my daughter, a friend and I

9

were doing something and my friend said something about a situation that was, "as serious as a heart attack". I caught my daughter out of the corner of my eye and could see her body stiffen. I knew, and so did my daughter, that our friend didn't say that to be mean, it was just a descriptive phrase she was using. I also know that if either Courtney or I had said anything to her, she would have been devastated at hurting us. Sometimes, although it will be very hard, it's best to just be quiet.

If someone called and asked if I wanted to go to dinner, I said yes, but I made it a practice to ask where they were thinking about going. If I knew it was some place that would cause a "memory" I'd either make an excuse, or suggest a different place. It was an easy excuse to suggest a different kind of food, we do it all the time, and no one thinks a thing about it.

There will be some big triggers that, unfortunately, you are just going to have to deal with. The holidays, birthdays, your anniversary. My suggestion for these is not to make major changes in how you celebrate them, but instead make small changes. Have the same menu, but let's say you always put out a relish tray at Thanksgiving because your spouse or partner loved it, even though you didn't. Well, drop the relish tray.

One of the things I did with my daughter at Christmas was to take a tag that was for an older boy, or man, off the giving tree we had at church. We made it a point to buy everything on that person's wish list, and if the list was short, we'd add a few things. It felt good to be shopping for men's things, just as we would have if John were alive, and I knew that it would make him very happy to be able to help someone. Those shopping trips also gave Courtney and me time to have a normal "shopping" conversation and buy things that "dad would like". And yes, when we were buying for that other person, we used those words, "what dad would like". Because the tags don't usually specify colors for the clothes on the list, we bought things that would have looked good on John, and while we were shopping, we would often comment that the item would have looked good on him, or brought out his eyes; normal comments we would have made anyway.

On our anniversary I made it a point to celebrate by taking friends to something special. For a few years it was a fund raiser called "Men Who Cook". Prominent men from our area would donate time and product to make all sorts of dishes that you could sample for a set fee. I always made it a point to take care of the elephant in the room by telling the people I invited that this was to celebrate my anniversary. On what would have been John's birthday the children and I went out to dinner and raised our glasses to him in a birthday toast.

Celebrating like this, helped me to face the biggest hurdles head on, and softened the pain that came with them.

Once of the biggest and hardest things you will do will happen within a few weeks of his burial; going to look at the tomb stone or plaque. Just looking at a piece of rock or metal with his name and the dates he lived on it is hard, especially the first time and maybe a few times after that. I preferred to do it alone, but don't be afraid to ask a close friend or family member to go with you. My children went without me, and Courtney was seen more than once sitting on the ground by the headstone reading a book. Bring a chair if you want to do something like that, there's nothing wrong with doing that, and a chair will be easier on your body! I've noticed in more than one cemetery there are stone benches in memory of loved ones. I was very moved to see coins on John's stone a few weeks after we buried him. Some of Courtney's friends are Jewish, and had left the coins to tell her that they had gone to see her dad, and that he wasn't forgotten.

HOW LONG WILL I FEEL LIKE THIS?

Your partner or spouse was an integral part of you. It may have been for a short time or for many, many years. There is no correlation between how long you were together and how long you should grieve. But, don't making grieving for the rest of your life a goal. Take it day by day and allow yourself to enjoy life without feeling guilty. Yes, you should accept those moments of intense sadness, but they will grow farther and farther apart as time goes on. Notice I said farther apart, not that they will disappear entirely. Don't be shocked if years down the line something triggers that feeling. Just know that if you allow it to, it will pass. My grandmother was visiting us one time and she started talking to John about her husband, my grandfather, who had been dead for at least thirty-five years at that point. Before either of us knew what was happening Grandma Rose was sobbing and going on about how much she missed him. At the time I didn't understand, but I do now, and you will too when you go down that road.

WHAT ARE YOU GRATEFUL FOR?

Several months after John died, I changed jobs and spent a lot of time working out of town. My son Joe had graduated by then, so after work he was home with Courtney, and could be there for her at night until I could get home. Even if I spent the night in Ithaca, the city I spent a lot of time working in, Joe was home with Court, making sure she did her homework, someone made dinner and took care of her needs. Often, I would work until midnight, and then leave again at 7 or 8am. Of course, I was running away.

One time I mentioned to a friend that I was thankful for the zip strip on the side of the road, because there were times, I dozed off on my way home and that strip did its job and woke me in time to prevent an accident. I went on to say that even if I crashed it would be all right because I'd be with John. She chided me and asked what Courtney would do without me. To that, all I could say was that she had three brothers who would take good care of her, but it did tell me two things. First, I had a daughter to live for and finish raising, and second, I was really a lot more depressed than I was admitting to.

In retrospect, I should have sought professional help, which probably would have gotten me to a better place faster than I did on my own. Instead, I started a journal that I forced myself to write one thing I was either grateful or thankful for daily. In the beginning I really had to search for things to write about. One or two lines was fine, and I repeated some things, like my children or a really awe-inspiring sunset. It took a few months of writing, but it gradually became more natural. I went from having to search for something to be grateful or thankful for to finding more than one thing a day.

In the meantime, my daughter joined a group at school whose members had lost someone close to them. They met for a few weeks, and then the group was discontinued because it got too big and didn't have enough advisers. She felt it helped her a lot to be with people who had also lost someone close to them and to talk about her dad, but she didn't want to go to a therapist when that group ended. I think as a parent that maybe I should have insisted; and would have if I had been in a better frame of mind myself.

But this brings up my next point. You can't go back and do things differently. You should have made sure so and so knew and came to the funeral; you wish you'd had him wear something else; why didn't you use this reading instead of that one. The list of should haves and would haves can go on forever, but you did the best you could at the time. Stop chastising yourself, it's not doing any good and is only giving you something you can't do anything about, to dwell on.

MONEY, CREDIT CARDS, INSURANCE, ETC.

Don't accept "no"! After your spouse or significant other passes, there will be a lot of things to deal with. I'm not talking about things attached to the burial; will he be cremated or buried, what outfit should he wear, etc. I'm talking about credit cards and loans, the cable, phone and electric bills. These are just a pain, but they have to be dealt with! When you call these companies depending on who is on the other end of the line, it will either be a very good experience or just plain awful! The person on the other end has either dealt with this before; or makes it very clear that they don't want to. When you get someone who doesn't want to help you, you have a few options, and one of them is *not* to give up. I called a credit card company three times before they agreed to apply the insurance; I paid for years to pay off my card in case of death. The first person told me I didn't have insurance, even though I was looking at it on the bill. The second person agreed I had insurance; but said it didn't apply to the second person (in this case my husband) on the bill, it would only apply if I was the one who died. The third person agreed I had insurance, that it covered both John and me, and they took care of putting through the necessary paperwork. As I said, it all depends on whom you talk to.

Be persistent! Recently I spoke to a woman whose husband had passed away something like 10 years ago. She said she wanted to change her cable plan but couldn't because the bill was still in her husband's name, and the company wouldn't allow her to change it to her name. What they apparently hadn't explained very well was the procedure: She would provide proof of his death (what this proof is varies from company to company), then they would close the old account, and open a new one in her name. Instead, here she is 10 years after his death only being able to watch the channels, he chose years before! Sometimes these "customer service" people make it sound as though it's a huge deal to do something when it really isn't. Keep in mind that this is something they are paid to do, and something that will make your life easier. You are the one who counts! It may seem easier to just let these things go, but you should deal with them as soon as you can.

If you have a friend who would be willing to make a call you can't handle, give them your information and set them free to handle it, or put the phone on speaker and tell the person on the other end that this person is with you and can speak for you. Honestly, it's easier if they just portray you though. The problems with just accepting and living with, or leaving whatever it is in his name is two-fold. First, every time the mail arrives and there's something addressed to him it will hurt and be a reminder that he is gone. You don't need a daily reminder; you'll have enough other things that will trigger that memory. The second thing, is when you have a problem, or like my friend who wanted to change the cable stations she got, it will be more complicated. Change these things as soon as you feel you can mentally and emotionally. Just because you don't see insurance on a bill, don't assume you don't have it.

Did you know that insurance covers Parent Plus loans automatically? Did you realize that many bank loans have automatic coverage? My son is a loan officer for a credit union. Recently he assisted someone whose spouse had been very ill and was hospitalized for a prolonged period time, to file for insurance on loans they had. These people didn't know they had insurance and had been struggling to make payments every month. He got back hundreds of dollars for them and saved them thousands more. Always ask, and if the answer is no, ask again, and maybe a third time.

Speaking of money, death certificates cost money. You will need a couple to start with, but you can always get more as you need them. In New York, one of the ways these are obtained for you is by the undertaker, other states may have different procedures. Either way, you can always get more. Don't put out money you don't have to because many places will accept a copy without a raised seal, and copies are really cheap! One place I contacted just looked up the obituary. Don't assume that every place will need an original certificate. Whatever you do, keep an original with your important papers, for yourself, you never know when you will need it, so it's best to have one handy.

After a certain amount of time monies in bank accounts, safe deposit boxes, pension funds, apartment deposits etc. will be considered unclaimed and are turned over to a state government agency. The money that is turned over to the state is not lost forever, but once it's turned over, you have to file a claim to get the money. These monies are posted publicly and anyone can check to see if they or someone else has money sitting dormant. To do this all you have to do is Google "unclaimed funds" for any state. You should do this every so often. Some of these funds don't have to be turned over for up to five years after they are considered abandoned. You may have a windfall waiting for you to claim it. Of course, it could be $5, but what the heck, it's your money! Be sure to check multiple states because the account will be turned over to the home state for the company. For example, let's say you live in New York, but he went to school in Massachusetts. When he was going to school, he put down a deposit on an apartment, where he lived for a couple of years. He was young, and didn't realize he needed to request a refund of that deposit, so when he graduated, he just moved to New York and started working. That deposit could have gone to the Commonwealth of Massachusetts, and that is where you need to file your claim.

When my father died, we found a safe deposit key, but no identification as to which bank it was from. And of course, when we called the banks, even though we explained the circumstance, they couldn't give us any information because our name wasn't on the box. About six months later we got a bill for the box from a bank, so that solved that problem. Unfortunately, in this day and age many of our bills are paid by automatic withdrawals. I'm not sure my children would question a withdrawal labeled "bank service" and may miss something like a safe deposit box.

These automatic withdrawals bring up another problem. They are great at making sure a payment is never late and that your husband never had to write a check, make out an envelope and find a stamp every month, or quarterly, semiannually or annually, *but* that company will also continue to make the withdrawal until someone tells them not to. What this means to you is that you may be paying for something that's no longer needed like an insurance policy or even a magazine subscription.

It's funny, John and I were very close, but when he died, I felt like I was doing something wrong looking through his wallet. I don't think I ever did that in all the years we were married.

You may feel that way about looking at his emails, or accounts, but at one point or another, you will have to if nothing else to make sure there aren't any monies being withdrawn automatically. If you find a bank account that is incurring fees for one reason or another, like inactivity or again, automatic payments and it's overdrawn, contact the bank or credit union immediately.

WHAT! HE DIDN'T HAVE A WILL?

A friend of mine just lost her husband. In talking to her I found out he didn't have a will. This makes things so much harder on the family! He didn't have any children and he had a very small estate (well under $50,000). In New York things that are jointly owned pass to the spouse, but God forbid he should have anything in both their names, but I digress, anything not jointly owned goes through the courts. She was going to call her lawyer, at how much per hour, to handle the paperwork. I suggested that she call her local county clerk and I explained to her that in New York State there is a form you can file to name yourself as administrator for small estates. The form cost her $1. That's right, $1. I'm sure most if not all states have a similar process.

So, she made a phone call or two, paid her dollar and took care of the filing herself, and in the process saved herself hundreds of dollars. It's your money, you can throw it away any way you want, but I'd rather spend it on something else instead of a lawyer's fees. This also brings up the reason for you to either make or update your will. It's not hard, nor expensive, but it will help the people you leave behind.

THINKING ABOUT RUNNING AWAY?

It can be very tempting to move someplace different. You look around and see memories everywhere, every memory rakes up something from the past and can cause pain. But keep in mind that those memories can also rake up something happy from the past. One of the moments you don't want to lose. I'm not saying that you should never move, but I would suggest staying put for the first year or so. You have friends and connections where you are. These are the people who were there with you while your spouse was sick, or dropped everything and were there for you if his death was sudden.

While it's great to move to be with family, sometimes it's better to stay and be with contemporaries who understand who you are today. Many of these people have suffered losses just like you, and although they will all have advice, they are willing to share, which can drive you crazy, they may very well understand you better than the family who really knew you a long time ago, but not so much now.

THE KIDS AND THAT INHERITANCE

Now, please understand, this next comment isn't meant to reduce your loss to dollars and cents. You may find that financially you are better off now that your loved one is gone. Every person's circumstances are different. I was a young widow with relatively young children. We had depended on both paychecks to make ends meet. However, when John died, some of our debt (read monthly payment) was reduced by the automatic insurance on that debt. A Parent Plus loan, a home equity loan, and a credit card were gone. Thankfully, I received a Social Security payment each month to help raise Courtney, and of course we were now down to one car to put gas and oil into and to insure. Financially, things were similar to what the budget looked like before John died, in fact just a little bit better. Obviously, I would rather have struggled with him, instead of doing a little better without him.

In the case of the person reading this, you may have insurance, you may have been spending huge amounts to park your car and visit him in the hospital, or he may have had a very expensive hobby that's gone now. Take a few months to let things settle down so you can see where you really are financially. Also, if you have a large influx of money, say via insurance, a retirement account, a bank account in his name only or something else, just let it sit for a few months. Don't be pressured by the people handling the money right now, none of those things I just mentioned have to be handled immediately. Do not feel obligated to "help the kids" or pay off every debt you have. First, you made it on your own, let the kids give it a try. They are adults, treat them that way. This may seem harsh, but I think of it as reality.

I have four very successful children. Do they all make six figures? No! They are all gainfully employed, or at this time, in the case of my daughter, at home raising one of my grandchildren, they contribute not just money, but themselves to help others and they are constantly setting good examples for those around them. Oh, yes, and they have all found that they don't have to have designer everything to make their lives complete.

If that isn't the case with your children, it is in their, and your, best interests to set them free and see how they do. You raised your own children, let them raise theirs. Are they struggling because of their lifestyle or yours? Chances are that the problem is with their lifestyle or mindset toward you. It is not your responsibility to continue to take care of them. It is not their right to bleed you dry. If you have any lump sums of money come in, first, don't tell them and second, put it into a short-term CD at your bank or credit union. In six months or a year when it matures you will have a much clearer head and make better decisions.

Also, if you don't have a financial adviser start by talking to someone at your bank or credit union. That person probably has seen a lot and can give you good common-sense advice. After talking to them you can decide about hiring an advisor. Your friends can also give you recommendations. Ask if you can have a free first meeting. If the person says no, find another one. If you don't feel completely comfortable with that person, find another one. Don't short change your instincts. This person will have your financial future in his hands, so if you have any reservations, look for someone else.

And let me say it again, don't be your children's bank; no matter what happened in the past or threats they make about the future, it is not their right to take your money! Understand that there are people, maybe your children, who will threaten you with things like, "you will never see your grandchild again" or "if you don't help us, our lights and heat will be turned off". Let me say it again, don't bow to threats like these, and the many others that someone who is willing to use their own children, your grandchildren, as a bargaining chip. They will find a way, and as cruel as it seems now because after all, you have money and they don't, they are adults and need to grow up, not sponge off you. Stand firm, don't be guilted in to anything. They think you were a lousy mother, maybe you were, but throwing money at them now won't change those feelings on either side. Your guilt won't go away, and neither will their resentment or criticism. Those feelings, and probably criticisms will continue and just like blackmail, will never end. At the most volunteer to watch the grandchildren one, maybe two days a week.

You will be surprised at how many things you have on your plate to fill your days, and don't add a full-time babysitter to it. Many of you will say that you enjoy watching the grands, I love watching mine too, but unless it's something you did before grandpa died, don't start it now. This would come under the category of a major change of lifestyle and now isn't the time for that. If in six months or a year, it's something you really want to do, and can afford to do, consider it then. Don't let the parents present it to you as something that will "help you to deal with Dad's death." Trust me, you will have plenty to do without chasing the grandkids around.

I've talked to a few widows who found they were a little short of cash and wanted to take on a part-time job. This may not have been apparent to them right at the beginning, but a few months down the road when the tax bill came it or the holidays suddenly appeared on their calendars, they realized a temporary part time job could help. If they were watching the grandchildren every day, they wouldn't have the ability to take on a job. You need to remember that although your family lost an important member, you have too, and you need to be there for yourself first. This is not being selfish, it's being practical.

John loved spending time with the children

Left to right, Joe, John, John Jr. and Jim

1989 John Jr., Joe, Jim, Courtney, me and John

John and Courtney, not too long before his death

John

Life goes on. Jim, Courtney, John Jr., me and Joe

THOSE TOXIC, *HELPFUL* PEOPLE

At one of my jobs, we had what we called "gravity issues." These were things you couldn't change, like gravity. Your situation, of being left to fend for yourself is a gravity issue. You can wail and moan and go through all the stages of grief twice, but you are still a widow. We no longer have to drape ourselves in black veils for a year or cloister for that same amount of time. Unfortunately, this has led to the impression by some that we are no longer mourning, and that can lead to some very hurtful comments. The good news is that usually these comments aren't really meant to hurt. If there is one person in your new life who is particularly toxic and is making comments that bother you on a regular basis, avoid them as much as you can. If you can tell them in a nice or semi-nice way how much these comments hurt, then do that. If you can't bring yourself to say something, then either take a break from being with that person, or enlist another friend to help you.

When John and I were married a good friend of mine told me that on my wedding day everyone would want to do something for me, so if I needed anything, all I had to do was ask. After you lose your spouse or partner you will find everyone wants to do something for you, so if you have one very obnoxious person that needs talking to and you can't do it, enlist the help of one of those people who have told you to call if you need anything. Obviously, you should choose a closer friend, rather than the neighbor down the street, but this is where you could use a mutual friend to help shut down the hurtful comments.

Also, don't feel as though it's okay if it's a relative making the comments. Even your own family doesn't have any right to judge you. Many of these people may have been through what you are going through right now, but this is your grief, and you have the right to handle it in your own way, and how you deal with it is none of their business!

GUILT!

Don't feel guilty! You didn't push for him to see a doctor, you didn't visit him enough in the hospital, you should have made sure he was taking his medicine, you didn't say "I love you" enough or the last time you talked to him. Why didn't you do this or that. Or even if you have negative feelings, don't feel guilty. When he was alive, you thought he was a miserable person and the world would be better without him. The list can go on forever. Face it, we are human and we make mistakes, we say things we shouldn't, and we don't say things we should. We've done that all our lives, but the difference is that the person we did it to, didn't die. Now you're a widow, it will seem to you that you committed the worst sin ever. You haven't, you didn't, and even if you did, you can't change it now…for that person. You can learn from it and be more attentive to others in the future, but you can't change what happened or didn't or what you said or didn't.

My John was one of the kindest people in the world. He would do anything for anybody, and there were times I said or did things that weren't nice, and I know made him unhappy. I certainly regret these things, but I recognize that there isn't anything I can do to fix them, except to learn by them and be a better, more caring person in his honor.

After John died, my daughter and I were talking and she said it was a shame he died when he did because he was just learning to say no and I was just learning to say yes. I found that to be great insight on her part and I took those words to heart. Now I like to think that I'm not always the "no" person, but rather the more thoughtful person. I also know that even John could probably find a regret or two if I were the one to die and he was still alive.

FORGIVING YOURSELF

I heard a long time ago that we can forgive anyone but ourselves. It's as though humans love to carry guilt around with them. We seem to thrive on it at times. Feeling guilt only makes us unhappy. You need to recognize it and make changes going forward.

It was December 1997 when I first realized that John had something going on and needed to see a doctor. We didn't have insurance; my plan that would cover the family would kick in January 1, 1998. We talked about it and he said he would make an appointment for a checkup in January. I mentioned it again in January or February. He never made the appointment and he dropped dead of a massive heart attack in March. For a while I carried the guilt of not making him call the doctor, or making the appointment for him. It took me quite a while to come to grips with the facts; John knew we had insurance, he was an adult and he could have made the call himself because he knew how he really felt and I was his wife, not his mother. If you feel that guilt weighing you down and making it difficult to even try to live life more fully, see a professional and listen to what they have to say.

A friend of mine has been talking to a therapist for years, and still carries guilt around with her like it's her job. She is very good at talking about her problem, but I'm not sure she's listening to either herself or the doctor. Unfortunately, many of her friends have decided that we'd rather stay away from her instead of listening to her go on and on about her regrets. We all have them, but there is a point in this healing process when we have to say we tried and we did everything we can and now we're going to pack them away, just for now and move away from them. We won't forget them or leave them behind, but we'll just acknowledge them and let them sit out of our immediate view for a while. Maybe the next time you visit them they'll seem smaller and less significant.

SURPRISES AND SCAMS!

Death can bring many surprises. From the gift that was purchased months ago for your birthday, to finding out that he left everything to his children from his last marriage. A woman living down the street from me found out after her husband died, that he had left the house they had lived in for several years to his daughter from a former marriage. The daughter gave my neighbor a few weeks' notice to pack up her things and move out. I wasn't close to her and, in fact, heard most of this story through the neighborhood grapevine, but apparently, she didn't have any idea that this was going to happen until it did. Surprise! You just lost your husband of many years and now your house is going to go too! She fought it and lost. Not a nice thing for the family to do to her, but it happens. I think she did the right thing in fighting it and hope that if you find yourself in that position you will fight too.

This brings to mind the many scams that come with the death of a loved one. A very old one is when you get the letter, or today it might be an email, telling you that your loved one purchased something from a company (the original scam was a bible) that had been bought, but it was never paid for. No matter how legitimate the letter or email looks, do not send them any money! Make them send you proof of their claim, what they sold, when it was delivered, how much it cost, how much has been paid already, and even then, do not pay it! Wait until you are thinking more clearly.

Look into all claims, no matter how much they are for. Look into all companies claiming you owe them money, many of them are fraudulent. If a company has a real claim to money, you can probably find something in your house, like the item or a statement, or some kind of paperwork relating to that claim. Even if it is a large well-known company don't assume you owe them money. Even if the company is threatening to sue you, do not pay it until you are 100 percent certain you owe that money. Don't let them frighten you into paying.

IT'S TIME TO LEARN
WHAT YOU CAN DO

You are stronger and more capable than you think you are.
Years ago, I was the manager of a temporary employment service. We had a lot of women come in looking for jobs after their husbands had left them, or had died. I always tried to interview these women out in our waiting room so that it was a more informal setting. Many of these people hadn't had a "real job" in many years and when I asked them what they could do, most said that their skills were way out of date and they didn't think they could contribute much to the corporate world.

After hearing this I often asked them what they did at home? Did they schedule the family's activities and make sure everyone got to baseball practice, doctor appointments, and their husband's work events? Did they take care of the checkbook and budget? Was it up to them to transport children here there and everywhere? How about meals? Did they plan them, buy the things to make them and then prepare them? In general, many who walked into my office thinking they were skill-less, walked out knowing that they could get a job and cope with their new life.

You can do the same thing. You have many, many skills, and when you believe that you can add to those skills. If you are not familiar with computers; go to the library or OASIS, or your local high school or community college and take a class. It's not hard, and will only help you in the end. You may also meet some new people too. Remember we talked about not paying a claim until you researched the company? The internet is the place to do that. Afraid of computers? There was a time when people were afraid to have a telephone in their houses, but then they found out how useful and fun it was to pick up the receiver and talk to someone. You will find out that the internet is the same way.

Google and I are best buddies. I can ask Google anything and it doesn't mock me or ask why I want to know that; it just answers my questions. I can look up recipes, find out when a company was founded or what the King of England is doing today. Yes, sometimes I go down the rabbit hole and get carried off into realms of cute puppy pictures, but usually I can find out what I need and go to my task quickly. I could go to the library and pore through stacks of books and magazines, but time is valuable and all that takes time. You were left here to carry on; use your time and money wisely.

After John died, one of my kids asked (and I chose to think he was being funny) who was going to sew the buttons on their shirts now that Dad was gone. I really don't like sewing, so I never admitted that I could do minor repairs including buttons and hems, and John took care of those things. Now that he's gone, guess who had to fess up to being slightly proficient with a needle and thread. I also have made You Tube an acquaintance.

A friend mentioned that she had to call a locksmith because she had lost the key to one of her doors. I suggested that she buy a new knob set and put it on herself. The knob wasn't anything out of the ordinary, so it could have been easily replaced. She looked at me as though I had two heads! I'm sure replacing it herself would have cost a quarter what she spent on the locksmith and that's factoring in her time doing the replacement, driving to the hardware store to pick up a new set, and watching a short You Tube presentation on how to make the change. Maybe it's an age or money thing, but why not do a simple job yourself? You'll be surprised at the satisfaction you get from it.

Take the experience one step farther and use the money you saved to take a friend out to lunch and brag about what you did all by yourself! Trust me, she'll be impressed! Recently, I called a well-known company to block or repair a basement window. I didn't care how it was fixed; I just didn't want cold air coming in. They wanted $400 to fix it! My son invested $17 in materials and less than an hour of his time, and voila it's fixed! I hadn't even looked at it, but based on what he said, I could have done it myself. Thank heavens, I didn't go with that company!

Another place where you can find tons of help for some of the minor, but costly repairs around the house, is your local either family owned or big-box hardware store. You will be surprised at how knowledgeable and helpful most of the sales associates are. And, if they find out that you're a widow, often they will go out of their way to assist you. Take advantage of their expertise, and after listening to them make the decision whether to hire someone to do the job or try it yourself.

IT'S OK TO TALK ABOUT HIM

In talking to some widows, I've found that they are hesitant to mention their husbands. If he were still alive, I know his name would be sprinkled throughout the conversation, but now that he's gone, they feel awkward saying his name, even when it would be completely natural. An example would be if you were talking about a particular place you're going, the other person may say something like, "John and I went there and really loved it", or "that was one of the places John and I always wanted to go to."

In the beginning he's on your mind constantly, and even after many years you may think about him often. It's okay to include him in your conversations. One of the things I really miss about John being gone is that I can't introduce him to the people I know now, who never had the opportunity to meet him. I think that in a way, when you mention him, you are introducing him to your friends and you are saying what a great guy he was, and that he's not forgotten. I also think that for those who are uncomfortable that you're widow, it breaks the ice and gives them permission to talk more freely about their spouse. In a way it shows them that you are all right discussing your loss. For me, John was an integral part of my life when he was alive, and I feel as though he still is when I say his name.

I have found it interesting how people you don't know react when you play the "widow card". I haven't done it deliberately very often; usually it's accidental. What do I mean by the widow card? When you are talking to somebody and you mention you are a widow, often their attitude and how much they want to assist you changes, and they become 100 percent more helpful. My daughter and I were somewhere recently where I was trying to get some help with something. I (very innocently) said something about how John would have handled the problem if he were alive. Immediately, the person working with me became my knight on a white horse! His attitude was suddenly one of caring and helpfulness.

Afterward Courtney looked at me in complete awe at the change that had come over him. She thought I used the "widow card" on purpose. Using the "widow card" isn't the same as keeping him alive in conversation, but it's a handy tool for when you really need help that you're not getting. Just keep in mind that you are not proclaiming something, but rather just mentioning it at the right time.

As humans we tend to project our feelings onto other people. I have friend who will often tell me that something is too hard for me to do, when in fact it's not hard for me, but it is for her. The same thing holds true for our feelings. If the person you're talking to experienced a loss, whether it was a close relative or friend, they assume that you are handling your loss of your spouse the same way they handled their loss. If they are still mourning, even if they don't share that with others, they will feel a great empathy with you and project that onto you. I'm not saying you will feel the same way. You are different people and each person handles things and feels things differently.

Also, if this is a stranger, you have no idea who they are still holding onto, or what their loss was. In this situation follow your gut reaction. If they are just acting sympathetic, my advice is to accept the situation and let it go. If they mention a specific situation or person and you want to probe for more answers, go for it. You will know what to do when the time comes. Trust your instincts.

A VISIT

Several months after my father-in-law died my mother-in-law told us that she was selling the house they lived in since he built it for them right after their marriage. Although she knew she couldn't keep it up any longer and she needed the money the sale would bring in, she was unsure about her decision. Then one day she stopped by our house and while we were talking about the sale John and I could see that a change came over her. We could tell that she was calmer and very at peace with what she was going to do, so we asked her about the change. She very hesitantly told us that "Pops" had visited her one night a few days ago. It was at night, and he just stood in the bedroom doorway. He never said a word, but smiled and nodded his head "yes." Pops never talked a lot, and this is what he would have done if he were still have been alive. She knew that this was his way of telling her it was okay to sell.

Fast forward 20 or so years and I lose my husband. There were so many things I missed about him, and one of them was our nightly talks. We used to lie in bed and talk about our day, the children, any gossip we'd heard, future plans; nothing special, just quiet conversation. One night I sat down on the bed, and he was sitting next to me. We both reached out and touched fingers and just talked. To this day I can't tell you what we talked about, which is odd because it was such a momentous occasion, getting to talk to him one more time, but it was just…normal. When our conversation ended, I leaned over to kiss him, and that's when I realized what had happened, and that he wasn't there anymore.

John has made his presence known other times too. Once at a family dinner, my brother, mother and others at the table were engaged in a favorite pastime of our family, arguing politics. At one point someone "made a point" and the chandelier over the table blinked. It had never done that before, nor has it happened since. All talk stopped, and then we started to laugh. We all knew that John was enjoying the conversation and chiming in!

When my daughter turned 16, one of the things she asked for was to go to a medium. This was three years after John had passed away, and I was only in my mid-fifties and still wearing my wedding and engagement rings. I cautioned Courtney not to say anything about her father being gone. The medium went through a pretty standard reading, "a friend will ask you for advice and then not use it, so you will get mad at her" Duh, you think that might happen to a 16-year-old? But, as we were leaving, the woman stopped us and asked if Courtney had lost anyone significant in her life, because she was sensing a protecting presence around Court. Mrs. Walker, the medium, went on to say that this person was with her consistently and was almost guarding her. We both knew it had to be her dad.

Courtney is now married with a daughter of her own. When Daisy was maybe six months old, Courtney could see Daisy on the monitor, looking at a specific corner in her bedroom. She would periodically break into fits of laughter, as though someone was standing in that corner making funny faces to make her laugh. Grandpa?

My point is, seeing your deceased loved one isn't unusual, and if or when it happens, it's okay. I firmly believe our loved ones don't just abandon us if we don't want them to. Would I run to someone to try to contact them, no, I don't suggest that at all, there are too many quacks out there, but if it does happen, know that you are loved, not crazy.

LITTLE BIG THINGS;
SLEEPING, REMINDERS AND RINGS

Nights seem to be the worst times for missing our loved ones.
John and I shared a room and a bed, so after he died, I found it very hard to sleep without his body next to mine, or without his scent. For a while I just used his pillow and propped another one next to me to mimic his body in the bed. That did help. To this day, I have a partial bottle of his aftershave in a special place and every now and then I sniff it, even though it's been over 20 years since I lost him. Other widows I've talked to keep a special shirt or other piece of clothing near them at night to help them sleep. I really want you to know that this isn't odd, nor is it something to be ashamed of.

One of the harder things to do is to get rid of his clothes and personal items. His clothes can help someone else, but if you can't part with them, or need to see the closet full, by all means hold onto them. The funny thing is, is that when John was alive his things took up half the closet and mine, the other half. After I cleaned out his side, I moved some of my things over. Looking at my closet right now, I wonder how we ever shared that space. The same thing is true about his dresser. It's full of my clothes! Where did we keep these things when he was alive?

Probably the hardest thing for me to do was to stop wearing my wedding band and engagement ring. I was a widow for about four years when I realized that it was time to take them off. For me, every time I looked at those rings I thought of John, our engagement and wedding day. I could hear him saying "Forever and a day" in my ear, and it hurt. No other way to put it, it hurt more than anything else.

I talked to my daughter before I took them off and put them away. I did this for a couple of reasons. First, I didn't want her to think I was trying to forget her dad's and my time together and second, I knew she would understand that it would be a signal I was taking the next step, which was admitting he wasn't coming back. She and I went to a local jeweler and selected a small, simple ring with a heart shaped garnet in the middle. Garnet was John's birthstone. Although looking at it reminded me of him, it invoked different memories than the wedding set did. After just under 26 years of marriage I needed to have the feel of a ring on that finger, and that fit the bill. Unfortunately, the ring was lost (read stolen) during a hospital stay. I hope the person wearing it enjoys the same peace I did when I looked at it even though they won't see my husband or my daughter and me on the day I bought it. Like the aftershave I still go back to the wedding set every now and then and take a peek.

Another reason for taking the rings off is that it is a signal to someone new you meet that you aren't married. With the rings on, you run the risk of them asking what your husband does or thinks about something. It takes the pressure off your explaining you're a widow and their expressing condolences for someone they never met.

JUST ACCEPT THE PRAISE

I have always found it hard to accept praise. Maybe it's that Catholic "you can always find a sin to confess" mentality, but, although I know I'm a very capable person, it embarrasses me to have someone point it out. One of the things I've heard fairly often is how well I did raising my children. My kids are really incredible, but I didn't raise them alone. When John died our oldest was 23 and the others, 21, 18 and almost 13. For the most part they were either adults, albeit young adults or closing rapidly in on adulthood. You can see by their ages that I certainly didn't raise them by myself, John was a huge contributing factor! Over the years I have had to work very hard to tactfully say this to people. I'm still working on it. It's flattering to be praised like that, but I feel so phony just saying thank you.

You may have similar things that you will be praised for, or may have people telling you what a great guy your spouse or partner was. If he wasn't a great guy, what's the phrase, "street angel and house devil", it may be very difficult to hear this. It's probably best to just let them think he was wonderful and not say anything. I know it seems like a lie, but what's the point of shattering their illusion?

DATING

A few years after John died, I dated a couple of people. It was nice to go somewhere with a man; to have him hold doors, kiss me, and pay the check. I could feel like a woman instead of a mother. Both of the men I dated were very nice, but when I was with them, I almost felt as though I were cheating on John. In addition to that feeling, I had my daughter to consider. When John was alive, we discussed the fact that we both loved our children more than words could express, but, and this was a big but, we also knew that we would be together long after the kids left the nest. All right, we were really off on that one, and circumstances definitely weren't the same, so I really had to take my children's, and especially Courtney's, feelings into consideration. The boys were older, and honestly being boys, I don't think they took in the big, long-term picture. They were more like, "okay, Mom's seeing someone," not, "okay, Mom's seeing someone, and he could end up being my stepfather." Courtney on the other hand, was torn. She wanted me to be happy, but she didn't want her dad to be replaced.

One of the men I saw had a daughter and I could tell that she was thinking along those same lines. Although you can't allow your children to rule whether or not you date, you do need to take their feelings into consideration. After all, you were a family first, before this other person came along. The person that died was their father, or at the very least played the father figure role in their lives, so you have to consider their feelings and concerns. Admittedly, there are going to be situations where the children are protecting their own interests in the money you were left, or other property you have, but it also could be that they are seeing something that your love-blinded, lonely widow eyes are missing.

My advice is to take it slow and to discuss how they feel about your dating. If you have more than one child and they are older, I would talk to them individually. If your children are young, I would suggest you take it slowly and include them in outings so they can get to know this other person. Remember that even very little children have feelings you shouldn't ignore. If your children are small and still living at home it would probably be best not to cohabitate. If that person moves out, it will just be another man in their lives that has abandoned them. As much as you feel that you have to have a man in your life, think about the kids. Do they have to have another father-figure (and if he's living in your house, that's what he is), leave them? The real answer, even if you don't want to hear it, is no.

OUR CONDITIONING

My husband has been gone for 24 years, almost as long as we were married, and I can tell you that I still think about him daily. The difference between now and when I first lost him is that now I rarely feel grief when I think about him. Often, it's to tell him something or just a fond memory. I would be lying if I told you this happened over night, but I swear to you that if you keep plodding forward, one step at a time, you will eventually get to a place in life where you can think about him and the life you had together first without crying and then without feeling like there's a black cloud over you and then finally one day you will find yourself thinking about him and smiling.

I know this has already been said, but I think it's important to restate it. It's all right to accept the fact that he wasn't perfect. Just because someone dies doesn't mean that they are automatically the best person who walked the face of this earth, and didn't have any faults. Nobody is perfect, but when someone dies, we have the luxury of forgetting some of those faults.

Speaking of faults, there are going to be people who read this book not so they can help themselves get through their grief, but instead because they feel guilty about not grieving. Maybe the person you were married to wasn't a nice person, and in your heart, you really feel as though this world is better off without him. Not only that, but you feel like a fake accepting condolences and agreeing with people when they tell you what a great guy he was. That's okay too. From what I've seen of people in that situation, it's all right to let them say those kind words because it makes them feel better even if you want to write his name on a piece of paper, throw it on the ground and jump up and down on it. Even people I've known who didn't like their husbands, or were worn out from taking care of him and just felt it was better he'd passed on, still went through a grieving process. They may have skipped the anger and bargaining steps, but they still grieved. Unfortunately, they also seem to carry so much guilt because, we are conditioned that when your spouse dies you are supposed to feel sad, not relief. You are supposed to feel you lost something, not feel as though you're free from a great weight.

When new widows realize they are not really grieving it seems that they take on guilt equal to or more than the grief they think they should feel. If you are one of these people, please understand that you are still a good person even if you didn't love your spouse and don't miss him. Your biggest problem will be that you will probably move ahead with your life faster than some other widows, which may bring on even more guilt. Stop it! Stop looking for things to feel guilty about! Accept the fact that you have been given a second chance at happiness. Be grateful and go for it!

WEIGHT GAIN OR LOSS

One of the things I noticed several months after John died, was that I'd gained weight. I had always had to be a little careful, but in the year or so since he passed, I was probably 10 or more pounds heavier. I think that happened for a couple of reasons. First, the kids didn't care and John wasn't around to tell me how good I looked. Second, I wasn't eating right. None of us cared what we were putting in our mouths, so dinner turned into my just going through the motions and whipping up fast, easy, often high calorie meals. I think this is natural and what happens to many widows. They either lose a bunch of weight because they aren't eating, or pile on the pounds because they are just putting anything into their mouths. It happens, and like his death, it's not fair, but it still happens. The only reason I'm even bringing this up is so that you are aware, it can be fixed.

For those of you who gained weight, you can take it back off, just do it sensibly. Don't crash diet or do or take something that will be unhealthy.

For anyone who has lost many pounds, take a deep breath, and then vow to make yourself a decent meal at least once a day, and to eat higher calorie snacks a couple of times every day. If you've dropped weight because you don't like eating alone, either eat in front of the television, or look around and see if there is someone in the same boat you are and invite them to dinner.

Remember that once it was fun to cook, because someone (your spouse or significant other) was eating and enjoying your food. If you were someone who didn't like cooking or wasn't very good at it, but doesn't want to go to a restaurant alone, try taking a book and going early, when there are fewer people around and you can enjoy a quiet corner with a good author. Another place to think about going is to the movies where they serve meals. A comfy lounge chair, good food and a movie, that's doable alone or with a friend. You will find that once you start eating, food will taste good again and you will start looking forward to meals.

BE YOUR OWN PERSON

Your loss is just that, your loss. Others, friends and family knew your spouse or partner, but we all have different feelings and thoughts, so his death is different for each one of you. Don't let anyone minimize or try to tell you how to feel. If you want to allow other people, friends and family, to grieve with you, that is your option. It is not your responsibility to either share your grief or give them access to your feelings. Above all, it is not acceptable for them to tell you what you should be doing or feeling, no matter how well intentioned they are.

There will be people in your life who will assume that now that you don't have your spouse or partner to help you make decisions that you're now in desperate need of their advice. You are not in need of advice from a person like that. Don't let them convince you otherwise! You have seen the words, "You are stronger than you think you are" throughout this book. They are to encourage you. Hopefully, before you let someone into a decision, spend money, or make a major life change, you will think of those words.

GOING FORWARD

As I was writing this last chapter, I got a call from a friend of mine that her twenty-five-year-old grandson was cleaning his gun, and it accidentally went off, killing him. Twenty-five years old!

Last weekend, I went to the funeral of an old friend of mine. Although we lost contact in recent years, I still felt his loss deeply. As I looked around the church, what I didn't see were a lot of my old friends, and all I could think was, "Yup, it's starting."

What I'm trying to say is that death is a part of life. It's all around us, and if we don't watch out, it can envelope us, suck us into its black feeling of despair. The death of your loved one was traumatic for you and probably others. Death is like throwing a stone into the water. Your spouse or significant other is that stone, you're the first ring, the other relatives and friends are the next rings in the water. It's not an event you can or should ignore, but just as after that stone sinks and the rings stop forming, and the water smooths out, so too will your life smooth out - if you allow it. That stone will always lie there at the bottom of the water; it's not going to dissolve or disappear. The water will go on just as your life will; if you stop throwing stones.

As an old Catholic, I sometimes look back on the catechism lessons from when I was a child. One of the questions asked was, "Why did God make you?". The answer to that question was, "God made me to know Him, to love Him, and to serve Him, in this world and the next." Personally, I believe in God and heaven. It gives me comfort to think that I will see John sometime in the future. If religion is not for you, try to find something that will put you at peace with what has happened.

The only way you will find that "something" is to actively look for it, not by sitting there waiting for it to show up and pull you out of your despair. Think in baby steps. What can you do today? Don't try to build a grand plan that includes the next weeks, months or years. Focus on doing one thing that will bring even a small sliver of happiness to you or someone else today. Eventually you won't have to look as hard to find that one daily thing to do. Take baby steps until you can run from one happy moment to the next. It takes time, but it will happen.